BETWEEN SPACES

FRANCELI CHAPMAN-VARELA

Franceli Chapman Varela
Between Spaces
ISBN: 979-8-9905601-0-9

Book Cover Art: AnaMelissa Carrion (@anamelissatwice)
www.anamelissa.com

Book Cover layout and Logo Update: Jojo Sandoval

Manuscript editor: Roxana Calderón

Instagram: @celihangout @betweenspacespoetry
Website: www.celihangout.com

Soy Dominicano
by Dr. Francisco Chapman Veloz

Soy dominicano,
como el pendón de mi caña,
como el laurel de mi escudo
y el merengue que me baila.
Nombre ganado en batallas,
suelos henchidos de gloria,
Duarte grabado en el alma,
Sánchez y Mella en mi historia.

Soy de abril cancionero,
le canto también al mañana,
cuando el brazo y el acero
conviertan en bala la miel.

Al hablar del continente
mi canto es americano,
Pero el suelo de mi muerte,
me nombra Dominicano.

TABLE OF CONTENT

Foreword   8

Chapter 1 - Who Are You?   10

Raíces de Hatomayor   11
That's Not My Name!   12
It's a Dominican Thing   14
Three-Five   16
Soy Mujer   17
I Am Woman   17
Bronx   18
Around The Way Girl   19
Black Princess   20
Around the Way Girl Pt. 2   22
Between the World and Me   23
Desde Niña   24
Since I Was Little   24
Do I Matter?   25
Isms   26
Marker   27
America   28
Bill of Rights   29
Baile   30
Halones   32
Wild Fire   34
Rest   35

Who Am I?   37

Chapter 2 - Family Ties   38

Grandma's Hands   39
Hermana   40
My Brother's Keeper   41
Primo   43
Tías   44
Father Comes Home From War   45
April   46
¿Qué Comes?   47
My Sister   48
F A M I L Y   49

Chapter 3 - Lovers & Lies   50

My Little Mermaid   51
Knock   52
Manboys   53
#Yanomás   55
Help!   56
Sola   58
Que Rico   59
Frank   60
All Of The Lights   61
Blurred Lines   62
Lengua   63
¿Qué?   64
Piedras   65

Stones   65

Man Collection   66

The Struggling Friend   67

Sun Moon   68

2020 Two?   69

You Are a Gift   70

Perdón   71

My First Time   72

Teen Drama   73

Soul Ties   74

Broken   75

Rota (Broken in Spanish)   76

Love Writes Here   77

God Don't Play About Me   79

Write Your Own Vows   80

Love Lies Here   82

Chapter 4 - God & Truth   83

God Dream   84

Cambié   85

Grace   87

Deep   88

Memories   89

Award   90

From My Pain   92

Spoken Language   93

What Am I Resisting   94

My Teacher   95

Who Do I Pray For?   96

Trauma   97

No Ves   98

Made   9ⴹ

The Place   100

Sitting at The Dock   101

Preacher Girl   102

Stop and Stare   103

Believer   104

Woman at The Well   105

Sifting   106

Truth   107

Acknowledgments   108

About the Author   109

FOREWORD

Franceli Chapman Varela is my best friend. She holds this title, in part, because in the seven years we have known one another, she's become the person that when my soul's in a state of anguish or jubilation, I call or go see her FIRST: to share, confess, unload, seek guidance from or celebrate with. She's designated with the significance of being my ally, guide, and confidant, I believe, because we met during a season of great personal difficulty for me, and the very first thing we ever did together, when we were yet strangers, was pray. Now, that is a story for another time... but from our beginning, Franceli has been my safe space.

Safety is critical and a deep innate desire for all of us. Therefore, finding places and people where there is ease and room for us to be our most authentic self is a salve for the spirit. With Franceli there is no need for me to be anything besides me; as simple and complex an aspiration as that may be. In the course of our friendship, we have cultivated and been able to achieve closeness with deep authenticity and without filtering, even as we navigate the unsavory aspects of life and ourselves. We have sparred each other to greater achievement and goals. This poetry book is one of Franceli's goals as her late father, Dr. Francisco Chapman, held dual PhDs, was a greatly respected activist for the Dominican people, and was a published author himself. I have been there for the entire process of Franceli's sometimes arduous climb toward this achievement, and I am honored to champion its accomplishment.

Between Spaces is an anthology; a glimpse of the myriad of poetic narratives that many of us wrestle with, find ourselves in, or seek. It's an exploration of what it means to be human, a believer, Latin-a, woman, broken, validated, lost, triumphant, known intimately and ignored. Contained within the prose are affirmations and confessions longings and musings declarations and whispers from the heart. I think there is a place within this book where you will find connection and understanding as you traverse the prose. There is beauty and pain contained within. Now, I don't speak Spanish, and a few of the poems are solely in Spanish, so I couldn't understand what I was reading. Franceli was concerned that it would be alienating for me or other non-Spanish speakers. What I said to her was this in response: "I think it's humbling to know you can't understand something because you don't have the skill set, or because you weren't born in a place that has that culture. It's a moment of reflection that sparks humility. Subtle but powerful if you allow."

I hope you see the wisdom and humanity contained within these upcoming pages. I invite you to explore what resonates and perhaps find growth in what you don't understand or failed to comprehend. It is a place of entertainment, laughter, and mourning. I am thankful for the access I have had to explore some of these concepts in close proximity to Franceli; it's blessed me immeasurably. I am happy to facilitate this introduction to Franceli and her perspective to see what it sparks between spaces in your own heart. Enjoy.
Essence

Essence

CHAPTER 1

WHO ARE YOU?

Who am I
I'm always questioning
Finding answers in my history
Leaving more questions in my present
For my future me to answer
Who I am is ever evolving

RAÍCES DE HATOMAYOR

Raíces de *Hatomayor*
La tierra de mi madre
De esa profundidad
Creció un tulipán

Mujer valiente
Dentro de la tormenta
Dejó sus sueños atrás
Para darle a sus hijos más

A América van sin saber su lengua

La heroína de mis ojos triunfó
En un país extraño
Aprendiendo inglés
A los cuarenta y con fe

No hay ningún regalo
Suficientemente grande
Que pueda darte por los sueños
Que me ayudaste a vivir

Hoy espero que estés feliz
Tus sueños siguen
Viviendo dentro de mí

THAT'S NOT MY NAME!

I was born with this gift
From my parents it was given
It took me a while to even share it
I couldn't say it
I had to learn to frame the letters
Put them together
Once I could write it
I wouldn't stop signing
Signature upon signature
Until my hand would burn
Then my fire went out
I got quiet
People started to riot
Rebelled against it
Had their own suggestions
While I had a lot of questions
I never said them
I didn't want to make them
Uncomfortable
So I conformed
That became the norm
Of my gift
Hidden behind the shadows
In the space of my gap

As life kept making its laps
I couldn't stand on the path
Of their reprieve
I had to start demanding
Speaking
And shaking down the trees
I don't want my truth buried with my death
I want to die empty with nothing left
I want to share my truth
Boldly and unashamed
Even when I introduce myself
How I pronounce my name
I no longer spread the lie
That I have to say it in English
No short cuts or amending

I have stopped pretending that it's okay
There are dead men whose names are difficult
You found the time to learn theirs– right?
So why with my gift you put up a fight?

I'm not Fran or Franny or Chelli

¡Yo soy Franceli!

IT'S A DOMINICAN THING

Baked Mac and Cheese wasn't a thing
It was Velveeta and Kraft
Give my momma some slack
She came to America without knowledge of all that

It's a Dominican thing
That faceless muñecas
Ruled the living room and if you broke one
Watch your neck from getting smacked with a broom

So Dominican
Juan Luis Guerra might as well been the
National Saturday Soundtrack
For the fabuloso cleaning
Now as an adult I'm like yo
Those songs had so much soul and meaning
Now that's how I do my cleaning

It's a Dominican thing
I only like warm water beaches in the summer
With cold Maltas or *Kimalitos*
The only Country Club I knew growing up
Came in a glass bottle
I didn't know it was Frambuesa
At the bodega it was dame el rojo
—the red one
And after two sips
That sugar had us kids going full throttle

So Dominican
That I look forward to having tres golpes
And not three hits to the face
But the plantain
Egg
Cheese
Salami plate
—Hit with the vinegar lace...

It's a Dominican thing

———

14

That my Spanish is all chopped and scratched.
The Spaniards enslaved us and our slang
—Looked down at
But guess what ?!
It's the imprint of our ancestors ingrained in us
And that's facts!

So Dominican
I was never embarrassed
To walk around outside in a roller set
Or with the tubi and pinchos all around my head
It wasn't until my half Haitian friend taught me
I could wear a scarf instead

It's a Dominican thing
That my neck has a phantom pain
From all the burns from the blowers rage
Against my kinks the hot wind rained
La tias didn't understand
My hair was made to stand!

So Dominican
Jabón de cuaba was the laundry detergent
For the panties that hung in the shower
I thought it was normal for everyone
Until I noticed my college roommates
Didn't have the hand washing power

It's a Dominican Thing
The best part of Easter
Is the habichuelas con dulce
With the cookies with the holy cross
And how every holiday
birthday
baby shower turns into a turn up
—No matter the cost

So Dominican
That I travel like I'm going to church
Dressed to the nines
You have to be fly for all the clapping
that happens when you arrive

THREE-FIVE

3
    5

Three times I thought I don't want to be left behind

                                    Three times he spoke: the trinity started here
                                            have hope

Five lies
You are late
You aren't great
You will work till you break
No one cares what you make
Love isn't your fate

                                          Five truths
                                          His grace
                                          Enough
                                          His favor
                                          For me
                                        His Goodness
                                          Good
                                          My sin
                                        An offering
                                          His love
                                          Given

When you put them together what did I find?
Three-Five
Complete Grace
So run your own race
You will finish
You will win
No matter the pace

SOY MUJER

El espacio entre mis dientes grita poderoso
Mi cabello suficiente
Mis ojos profundos de compasión
Por el volumen de mi mirada
Mis labios cantan las alegrías y las penas
De mis antepasados abandonados en barcos
Tardé en ver que cada rincón y cada grieta
Debería estar ahí sin pedir disculpas

I AM WOMAN

My gap screams powerful
My hair enough
My eyes deep with compassion
By the bulk of my stare
My lips sing the joys and sorrows
Of ancestors dropped off in boats
It took a while to see that every nook and cranny
Should be unapologetically there

BRONX

It sounds annoying to some
                  But when I HEAR IT...
                                    I know
                                    I'm HOME
Shouted from across the street

                On the fire escape   and   rooftops

THIS IS HOW I'M GREETED!

When I say it

           You know the meaning

                        I'm Saying I'm repping

MY CITY
                MY BOROUGH

The longer you hold it the more
                THOROUGH

So the next time it rings in your ear...

Let the flavor of   Adobo   chopped cheese   and

                        nutcrackers ring!
Let the sound of timbs + fitteds sing

            The colloquialisms ring an anthem

                  Of the city that never sleeps
                        YERRRR!

AROUND THE WAY GIRL

Poetry in her eyes
Songs in her feet
You are more than
Around the way you see
Don't feed into what they say
There is depth to your grit
Purpose to your pain
The testimony of your story
will be someone else's gain

When you open your mouth they judge
The devil used it to shut you up
But God will give you a nudge
Calling you to be bold
Your authenticity will save souls

Your environment didn't make you
God did
You are more than the block you stand in
You stand on the shoulders of greatness
Through the fire your iron will sharpen
In the darkness you will rise

From the ashes you fly
So Go Girl Go!
No matter what you've been told
Around the way
Your life is worth more than gold!

BLACK PRINCESS

I love birthday invites
The ones with no ratchet fights
The ones that I get to dress up during the day or at night

My favorite invites are the kids parties or the ballet
Where I get to wear my tutu unafraid
Where I get to live out my unspoken and forgotten dreams

A prima ballerina she couldn't be
Dance classes were expensive
Wasn't born into a royal family
So I won't be addressed as princess
But the idea of both makes me really happy

I love being a black princess
Who's invited to the ball
Although I'm grown
Single
And with no kids
Can I borrow one to participate in the pageantry of it all?
So the moms don't wonder why is she here without a child
And having too much fun

I know
I know the wine
Candy
Karaoke
Face-paint
And bouncy house scene
May not be your thing
But here's a place where pretend is play
But in the play we believe
Believed to be kings and queens

The real world goes to dark rooms to pretend to have fun
Wearing the mask of confidence hoping to be liked by some
Took off our tutus and tiaras for a more "appropriate" dress
To be treated like a commoner at the square
What a mess

I want to be in high spaces with faces that regard me with pride
Not dark spaces where the real me has to hide
So call me weird
Silly or childish if you dare
I'm looking at the authentic spaces of joy
Which nowadays are rare

AROUND THE WAY GIRL PT. 2

I know the lies you've been told and fed
You will just be a product of your environment
You won't ever get out
Don't feed into what they say
They will have to eat the words out they mouth
I promise you'll get out—this isn't where you'll stay
Sooner than later the around the way will change
But your heart remains the same
Your word will still be your bond
You'll remain loyal and true
The hills and the valleys won't change the character in you
Ten toes down you remain
Despite the injustice against your person
Despite the come up
From stamps to riches
From buses to black cars
From bodegas to Catches
From grinding to relaxin'
The best thing about this around the way girl is...

You never lost her

With God you led her to the water

And from the fountain of abundance you drank
Breaking off the poverty mindset
Understanding no matter where you are
You never lack
So if you are shocked when you see me walking

Around our way
The flavor was brought
And as for how you can get it

I could never be bought

BETWEEN THE WORLD AND ME

Between the world and me
What did it mean
When I thought there wasn't a place for me
I wasn't ready
To not be
Black enough
Nor Latin enough

Caught up between two worlds
wanting to belong
Growing up was tough

My hair was too kinky
So they gave me a big cut
Then they criticized my "accent" saying
"Are you really "Spanish" or what?!"
Stop talking black
Stop talking rough
You're Latin?
You're not sexy enough

But wait—stop claiming black
Go back to your Latino camp
Because you have a language and country
You can go back
So why check the box that says black?

Divide and Conquer
This ignorance was wack
Now I'm all grown up
This vibrant woman full of swag
And I dare you to tell me that I ain't black!

DESDE NIÑA

Yo escribía desde niña
Las palabras entre las páginas
Me dieron la voz que no tenía
Ahora como adulta
Prefiero escribir antes que leer
Las letras se van formando
Dándome instrucciones
Cuando no sé qué hacer
Los versos en mi cabeza me van guiando
La poesía me lleva hasta las nubes
Ayudándome a entender
Las cosas que no comprendo

SINCE I WAS LITTLE

Since I was a girl I would write.
The words between the pages
Gave me the voice I didn't have.
Now as an adult,
I prefer to write than to read.
The letters will slowly form,
Giving me instructions.
When I don't know what to do,
The verses in my head guide me.
Poetry takes me to the clouds
Helping me understand the things I cannot.

DO I MATTER?

In this world of humanity
I'm trying to find my sanity
Between the shots and lock ups,
The stripping of rights
And the battles only women must fight.

Institutions have become ruthless.   The
welfare and health care of the 99 It's getting
harder and harder to find.

I'm feeling left behind,
Misplaced.
Erased from the history books.
How do I know where I'm going
If I can't find where I came from?
The trauma of the slave
Is the burden we all carry.

Finding a different fix
To satisfy the itch
Of what has been shattered...
I just want my life to matter!

ISMS

So many isms
Plaguing our humanism
But your criticism?
Are you truly warranted?
Don't you live in a glass house?
Full of Skeletons
You buried so deep
You pray no one ever sees
So now you project
And get all upset
Spewing your judgment
As you scroll
Being a troll
You feel justified tho
Believing some self-righteous
LIES!
I used to get angry and hurt by your ism
But God gave me new eyes to see
That your ism is your fear of inferiority
Your insecurity
Your limited vision of
God's abundance for me
I'm sorry that you don't truly believe
That it's for you too
So you crucify
Condemn
There is a lesson to pen about the
pandemic of isms that we fail to confess
Divisive behavior
Leaving the cruelty leeches to feast

MARKER

Moving in circles
Waiting in spaces
Hoping there's no eraser
To take me away
I want to be like a marker
Permanent
Makes bold statements
Fine line between humble
And
Left in the abyss
I don't want to dry out and be forgotten
I want to make a mark
Stand tall
Stand out
Not rooted in ego
Rooted in faith
To be my ancestor's wildest dream

AMERICA

Some of us become the seeds of the very fruit we disdain
The apple doesn't fall far from the tree
I didn't always have the meaning
Of which way the tree was leaning

Paternal or maternal problems
The sins of my father left me angry
While his legacy kept me fighting
For a piece of the American pie
That American dream is what was sold to the maternal side

My mom didn't have the tools to decide
It was as if her accent was a crime
All were created equal
I'm afraid not
But why?

BILL OF RIGHTS

Sitting at the counter of freedom
Listening to the whispers
Of those beaten and spat on
Feeling privileged to sit here
When the bill hits the table
I couldn't process how you thought
I would pay this check
I have the right to refuse to pay
The bill that has been laid
Let me explain
If what you put down
Was to get down and erased
The spaces and places
Where blackness creates
The meal you prepared

                          Has it

The beat in your hips

                          Has it

The indentations in your face

                          Shares it

Yet you think you have
The right to re-write it
The right to your own bill
Paying off expenses
Without paying debt
To the Lives that aren't kept
Your bill tells me it doesn't matter
So I'm leaving this table
Without paying a cent
Because our lives matter
And that's a RIGHT
I want you to never forget!

BAILE

Si me ves bailando
No estoy aquí
Me fui
Estoy en las nubes
Mis sueños existen en el baile
Y mis pies sobre el aire
Pasos sin coreografía
No quiero seguir a nadie
¡Esta danza es mía!

Durante la lluvia
En la cafetería
Recuerdos de bailes
En la galería mientras
El campo nos veía

Yo bailo donde quiera
Salsa
Merengue
Y bachata
De cualquier manera
Muevo las caderas

!Cuidado!
«La negra tiene tumbao»
Mira como se mueve esa morena
Movimientos y pasos
Para todas las quinceañeras

Siento la presencia de mis ancestros
En la fábrica de palo
El sonido llama mi ascendencia

Sin pareja
Prefiero bailar sola
Y a cualquier hora
Cuando extraño a mi padre
Bailo y siento su presencia

¡Qué alegría cuando

Soy el centro de atención!
En el baile sigo su legado

En el baile estás tú
En el baile estoy yo
En el baile sigo a tu lado

HALONES

¡Aguanté demasiados halones!
Pressed down so bad
I'm surprised there is anything left

Aguanté los halones
Caused by the fights
Broken furniture everywhere in sight

Aguanté los halones
From the tears my mother
Cried on my shoulders

Aguanté los halones
The jabs from the gossip

Aguanté los halones
Constant teasing
Fugly ugly
Gaptorious they called me
Pero mami me decía
Mi bella estrella

En el espejo
Veo los halones
Dejaron sus marcas
Sus manchas

Lo maravilloso de la resiliencia
Es que de las cenizas nos levantamos
Now I'm standing straight
No
I won't bend
And snap this tool for your rules
I cry out in anguish
Feeling unaccepted?
Adjust your crown!

Excuse me
I stand corrected
It was foolish of me

To even dare to try to
Gain your acceptance

WILD FIRE

Listen for a moment
Do you hear that?
The sound of Trauma
On her back
It's like that sound only dogs can hear
There is a space where she's deaf
But here
She hears
Loud and clear
The whispers of misters and misses
Their words chipping away at her
She remains quiet
Not wanting to disrupt
But the noises get louder
And when it creeps up
It bubbles and erupts
The rage spreads like a fire
Can't control the spread
Eating away at the forest
Of people standing in the way
Is like the wild cat that's been in a cage
It isn't until you see them in the wild
That you want them to be tamed
You can't quench this fire
Flames are ablaze
No longer taking the fertilizer you tried to feed it
Fighting back
But what happened to preventing
What created the wild to go
From beauty to flames

REST

RESTING in the abyss of busyness
What is this word, REST?

Why don't I have more of it
Why do I deprive myself of it
REST

Feeling lost in the stillness not knowing what to do
Because the value has been in the doing/pursuing

Not wanting to miss or be dismissed
Remembering all the times I was looked over
Treated like a pushover

Poverty wasn't my fault
So
I hustle
I grind
I'm trying to find freedom
Fight for it

Rest is a luxury I can't consume
I want to break the generational curse of being over worked

Papá me decía: I'll sleep when I'm dead
He's resting well now
A whopping 57 years of life
Was rest for him also out of sight?

I wonder as I try not to fall asleep standing still
Daydreaming that I had a rich dad that left me millions in a will
Is that a morbid thrill?

This is why I don't rest
Scared of the thoughts I have to reset
What are you afraid of?

Rest isn't bad
Yeah
Well
my identity got wrapped up
In what I did

So if I stopped
Who would I be?
Would I matter?
Would anyone even notice that I got caught
At the

REST

STOP

WHO AM I?

It's a Woman thing...

It's a Family thing...

        Nah nah
                It's a God thing...

Who I am   Who we are   Gets blamed on these

Gender vs Identity   Family vs Friends   Religion vs Politics

             Who are you?

    I'd like to believe I am the belief and understanding
           Of my experiences

What if I remember them all wrong

        What if the pain aids the pen to creativity?

Who are you without the pain

           I'm discovering myself everyday

CHAPTER 2

FAMILY TIES

Tied
Tied by Blood
Tied by Name

Personal Ties
Tied
To Laughter
To Love

Support
Tied
To Resentment
To Lies
Shame

GRANDMA'S HANDS

I always marveled at her hands
I've never seen them young

Man
Oh man, if those hands had a song
They would sing of all the prayers they've done

Of the mentas
Y galletas qué dan
Los esfuerzos y trabajo para recibir pan

She wore pants and worked the farm
She had the cojones to ask for a divorce

The blemishes that show me
The mark of a warrior
And veins that tell me she was tough

Now I sit here holding them for dear life
I know you fought the good fight
98 years young
I wish I asked for more stories
About those hands that survived and won.

HERMANA

Hermana
Sister
I used to watch Barney and cry
Not understanding why
Why we weren't close
I knew we had different mothers
But I didn't want you half the time
I didn't want to have a slice of you in my life
I wanted the whole piece of the pie
This was my thinking in my eight year old mind
The mountain we had to climb
To get to this place
Was like mount everest.
The climb was worth it

Pride and Ego had to be left aside
With long convos and tons of tears we cried
Having to work through
Lo que el espíritu mujeriego
El machismo
Y la perversión left behind
We both had so much trauma and scars
We both miss our daddy
His death hit hard
Apologies and therapy helped us get on track
Not to mention Jesus having our back
Our bond is breaking generational curses
And my prayer is that God reverses
All the ashes for beauty

I don't think I say it enough
I am proud of us

MY BROTHER'S KEEPER

Faith in Christ was the name that they gave you
Brother is what I called you
A gift
Dropped off by Santa Claus on Christmas Eve
I thought I was a mom at four
Changing diapers
I gave you bottles
Pushing the stroller
Full throttle
When the parentals would fight
You would run up to the attic and hide
Suck your thumb to keep your emotions bottled up inside

I played savior
Turned homework helper
Therapist
Nanny
And
Translator

Later
You weren't so small
You got really tall and when
voices and fists raised
It was an ugly exchange
I'm sorry I took out the anger I had for our dad
I became rebellicus and left
Started hitting the streets
Sneaking in like a thief in the night
I robbed us of brother-sister time
I ran away from my duties
Ran towards teen dramas
No longer wanting to be your momma
What if that wasn't the case?

You never saw me as momma
You saw me as friend
We played restaurant, school, and all kinds of pretend
What if what you wanted was an ally too
A place to place your feelings

The fracture of divorce
Took us down a course
I can't go back and change
Where did you place that pain

Do you resent me?
In the crashing of bodies when you played sports
Will you ever forgive me?
In the fog of the trees that you breathe

I'm walking on glass in the presence of Windex
Obsession with the mirror to be clean
Non-acceptance
Life is a teacher
And it feels like detention
A lifelong sentence
Hoping to uncover and heal the sibling wound
The things I consciously and unconsciously did to you
I take accountability and pray you do too
I pray you'll want to join me at the center
Fight for our better
I can't be the keeper on my own

PRIMO

Señor Chapman:

Hoy la novia llora porque tú faltas
Cuando te conocí ya era una adulta muy astuta
Estaba orgullosa de conocer al hijo
Del hermano que falta
Mi papá y tu papá eran panas
Cuando llegaban
Todo el mundo saltaba a sus pies
Hermano del primo José
El que siempre bailaba conmigo
Yo supe que conocerte sería genial
Y cuando llegué a tu casa
Me abrazaste como si nos conociéramos desde antes
Al tiempo nunca le diste mente
Con tu energía contagiosa
Y tu actitud positiva y vibrante
Un brillo
Un amor
Incluso amábamos al mismo equipo
Mayor de edad
Pero con espíritu de niño
Un oso de peluche
No pude hablarte en el idioma de nuestra patria
Un derrame te quitó la lengua
Pero no se llevó tu luz
Entonces
Un infarto te mandó al paraíso
Saluda a nuestros padres
A los tres
Te escribo en español
Porque sé que al marcharte
Con tus alas recuperaste tu sabor

TÍAS

Son las segundas madres
Son las mujeres
Que te celebran
Adoran y te dan dinero
Sus consejos no tienen precio

Ona
Nana
Hyta
Mi primera palabra fue de mi tía

Mayo y Carmen
El ritmo de la salsa me enseñaste
Estas conexiones me dan orgullo
Orgullo de ser tía

Ahora que soy tía
¿Cuáles serán mis lemas
Y recuerdos favoritos?

Tía de nueve
Quiero darle algunas veces
Lo que no se puede
Quisiera protegerlos
De los fracasos
Pero yo soy la Tía
No la amiga
Un día cuando ellos sean tío o tía

Pensarán en mí
La tía genial

FATHER COMES HOME FROM WAR

He left
Left to fight a battle
A WAR of regrets
I was 6
My heart has been at WAR ever since
And around it I built a fence
Became a man quick
To keep my loved ones in or was it out?
I've been having a lot of doubt
Will I turn out like him and leave for WAR too?
My fear is that I'd do that to you
Father never came home from the WAR
Left us to fend for ourselves
He called from the field and it was infuriating
This birth call is outdated
20 something years—
You think I sat by the phone and waited?

I've been too busy at WAR too
Not knowing how to forgive you
I have been waring ever since
I would make
My body available
But not my heart
Lies from abandonment disguised as protection
I left behind a trail of tears
Broken hearts
And some regrets
I lost some important people in battle
Running from pain
As I stare in the mirror
I see the scars
I didn't see them before
I was focused on the conquer
On winning the war

APRIL

The showers that came
Washed away the pain of the 2nd
The day of my father's birth
You see the memories of good times
Mixed with the bad times
Mixed with the sometimes
I wish he was here
The showers continue
To the 8th
No one on earth
Can ever take my momma's place
May these showers bring forth my flowers
Tulips

April
I cherish the day
Keys to my place
My Brother's face
A lover's taste
And all the other memories
This month brings
That I cannot erase

¿QUÉ COMES?

¿Qué comes?
Pregunta mi mai'
¿Por qué no comes?
Pregunta mi mai'
¿Quieres comer?
Pregunta mi mai'
¿No crees que deberías comer menos?
Pregunta mi mai'
¿No crees que deberías comer más?
Pregunta mi mai'

¡Ay, ay, ay!
Maybe me como una estrella
Para que me lleve lejos
De tantos «consejos»

MY SISTER

Here I am
But who am I?
Does it Matter?
Your story might as well be mine
I can feel your pain, your sorrow
I am woman
That is enough to tell you I love you
How could I hate you?
How could you hate me?
Oh I know!
Because you made man more powerful than we
You gave him the keys and let him lock it
He locked you into the prison
Of turning your back on your sister
For what?
For love?
Love transcends deeper than the lies in the words he tells you
This is my love poem to you
My sister
My love for you is great
Greater than his need for me to hate
Your hate for me fuels his tank
His tank to continue to drive all over your frame
My sister
When will you wake?
Your eyes are wide shut in the darkness of his night
But when the morning comes and you see the light
My arms will be here to give you fight

FAMILY

BORN TO	CHOSEN
LEGACY	DESTINY
HERITAGE	CREATION
BETWEEN THE WORDS	BETWEEN THE TIMES
WHATEVER COMES UP	WHATEVER WE HIDE

THESE ARE

TIES

CHAPTER 3

LOVERS & LIES

I'm a lover
Not a liar
So why do we lie to those we love?

MY LITTLE MERMAID

Is it Self-love or Self-Sabotage?
Looking at all this chaos
It's hard to tell the difference
With so much resistance

Am I over-correcting
For spaces and places
I had no boundaries
Is my self-love now too harsh
Like Rose thorns
Keeping your love out?
I want to bloom without hurting you
Without hurting me
Is it even possible to avoid casualties

Is this pain the buyer's fee?
The self work
To disembark from the toxic boat
And feel safe in yours

How can the heart distinct one boat from the other
When it can not see?
It just feels the familiar feeling
Of the rocking of the waves that make it sea sick
Maybe I'd be safer on land

Am I caught up in a fairytale
Of a rebellious daughter with daddy issues
Thinking a witch with your voice can save you?

Under the sea of darkness you can't find freedom
You have to love you the way you are
Search for the light within
That's a good start

KNOCK

There's a knock on my heart
Before I can even get up to answer
My mind is racing trying to figure out
How the stranger got past the security locks

I had my heart on full stop
Guarded like a Venetian vault
Yet God who fabricated and stitched you
Made sure you had the codes to get through

After the initial shock
My heart started to knock
Whispering morse code
To the places it failed
Waving the white flag for help

Then you started speaking
My heart's language
And the surgery began
Your words started to patch up
The open arteries
I had bandages for so long
I forgot I was bleeding

Time on the wall was lost
Don't even remember how long
Gods grace is what kept me
And I didnt bleed out
It may have taken long
It may have happened fast
But you were right on time
Now my heart can selah

MANBOYS

"Age ain't nothing but a number"
Was a song I would reference
As I changed the inflection in my voice
Trying to get noticed by a man
It was a lot
If I could rewind
Go back in time
And tell this young girl to stop
That this man is a bop
A Man he was not
Okay by stature and age he was
And frankly had no business being with you
Underaged
How child fetishes were engaged
Why wasn't I enraged?
By the smirks and the passes from this man-boy
Why did I crave for his affirmation?
I would tell her
Your daddy is a man-boy
Your brother's too
Dealing with daddy abandonment issues
And taking it out on you
I would tell you when you grow up
You will be disgusted
Baffled that you ever trusted
He was that into you
Age was just a number
Yet it still wasn't a pair
Because mentally and spiritually he's broken
To have such affairs
And when you grow up
It will be just as tough
Because now you want a man
Not just by the way he stands
Not the number on his checks
But by the handle he has on his cortex
His integrity
His character
Is he working on his traumas
Or does he want a girlfriend masked for a momma?

Does he love God and have a moral compass
Or as soon as things get hard
He jumps to his flesh?
Can you separate the men from the boys?
If all they did was swap out their toys
Now he's winding you up
Frolicking you around like a yo-yo
But when you need him
He's never around
He should have joined the Ringling Brothers
For the performance of this clown
Because even after all these years he's been crying change
Your frown hasn't turned upside down
This act has gone too long
Pack your bags and come on home
Leave the Peter Pan and the lost boys on the road

#YANOMÁS

¿Cómo te lo vuelvo a explicar?
Estoy cansada
De repetir lo mismo
¡Para!
No más
Acceso a mí
No tienes ya
¡Basta!
Las gafas color rosa
Están ahora rotas
Veo claramente
Ese amor ciego
Ya no existe
El amor que tengo ahora es propio
Este amor tiene límites
Abusaste demasiado de mi amor
¡Ya no más!

HELP!

I wish I could HELP

                                HELP you feel safe

Not knowing how to do it

                       How to HELP you get through it

                           I feel HELP less...

My anger is a cry for HELP

                          I'm annoyed, irritated and snappy

                              All because subconsciously

                        I don't know how to make you happy

                    I'm not a therapist or a doctor nor your pastor

I hope one of those could HELP

                          I wish when you looked at me

                            You didn't see inadequacy

                             Reflecting back at me

                              That's not what I see

I see sweetness

Integrity

                     And a little boy crying for HELP
Look up

        There is light at the top of your bottom

           Where you've gotten stuck

I'm sorry that I'm not equipped

I don't know how to climb in and grab you

But the angels can fly and if you ask them

I know they'll find you

If you put it on a map

The unhealed soul to the healed soul

Can be thousands of miles apart

How does your soul know where to go

How long would it take

To make it to our destination

Will I be there when you make it

Or maybe our souls have a different fate

Relinquishing control to figure it out

My prayer is that you'll be set free

From that ugly spirit that's kept you down

SOLA

Me estoy mirando en el espejo
No me dejes sola
He estado sola contigo en mi mente
En mis sueños he besado tus labios miles de veces

De vez en cuando
Te veo pasar afuera de mi puerta
¡ALÓ!
¿Me estás buscando?

Extraño tus ojos
Extraño tu sonrisa
Tú eres todo lo que quise

Mis brazos están abiertos
Porque tú sabes qué decir
y yo quiero escucharte tanto
Pero ya te fuiste
y me quedé sola con este querer

QUE RICO

¡Qué rico es el sonido de tu risa!
Las matas se mueven con más fuerza
Cuando tú pasas
Este amor sí hace falta
Amor inocente
Sin pruebas
Sin límites
Alcancemos las nubes
Vayamos lejos
Sin ir a ninguna parte

FRANK

Lo llevo por dentro
Pero muchísimas veces te lo voy a negar
No quiero que veas el trauma del amor
Que casi me destruyó
Y todavía está en mis venas

No
No
No
No lo puedo dejar
Me da fuerza para asegurarme
Que nadie pueda entrar
Es mi protección
La conciencia no tiene la razón

No me aconsejen
Ni me digan
« Ay
¿Y un hombre tú no tienes?»
¿Pa' qué?
Yo vi la oscuridad dentro la luz
Me llevó fuera de las fronteras de mi raíces
Pero no fue un paraíso
Aprendí a estar conforme en mi cárcel
Aunque sea así
Aquí nadie me molesta

ALL OF THE LIGHTS

Many have been blinded by the lights
By the action
Yet left with no satisfaction
To who and what they are

Don't forget
Of all the steps
Given and written
For you to get here

God created and fabricated an image
With no mistakes
So pump your brakes
Trying to belittle me
You may want to erase
that "little place" in me
Which is in you

I will stand by it and remember
Remember the dreams from the island
That lead my parents here
Remember the trials of the Bronx Bomber
The pressures that lead her here
Remember that the Hollywood lights didn't make me
And that the Lord always
Always favors me

BLURRED LINES

Keen sense of vision
Inferred & blurred in loss
I can't even begin to break down
To you what seeing from this lens costs
Would I see love more clearly?
Would trust come more easily?
Would life feel less weary?
Questions from other perspectives
Leaving a life of repentance
For choices made
Made from a jaded perception of reality
Taking L's like it's a formality
What a tragedy
Yet we all fall from grace
So
When the blurred vision
Causes us to fall
Take the plank out your eye
And dust yourself off
It's time to walk in your call

LENGUA

I want my lengua
To be like
Dulce de coco
Que solo sweetness
Comes out
Quiero que las palabras
Sean suave como el dulce
Entre nosotros
Ten cuidado
Language has power

¿QUÉ?

¿Qué dices?
What do you say?
Your words aren't matching
No me llegan con satisfacción
Signals crossed
Nuestras líneas tienen mucha estática
¿Qué pasó?
What happened?
I want to go back
To when the music of our voices
Was on the same track

PIEDRAS

Tiro piedras a luna
Porque quiero que llegue el sol
Quizá si la luna cae
Tendré más horas
¿Qué haría yo con esas horas?
Tendría más luz y gozo en mi alma
Más tiempo para alcanzar mis metas
No me apresuraría a correr
Encontra del reloj solar

STONES

I throw stones at the moon
Because I want the sun to come
Maybe if the moon falls
I will have more hours
What would I do with those hours?
I would have more light and joy in my soul
more time to reach my goals
I wouldn't rush to run
Against the sundial

MAN COLLECTION

Can we start a collection of men that are attractive
Not based on eye pleasing/sexual satisfaction
(although that's a plus)
Let the priority of the attractiveness
Not be distracted by lust

I want a collection of disciples,
Godly men
Who honor you, him and then me.

6'5 in the spirit tall and bold
Not afraid to speak the truth Wherever
he's told

Instead of dripping in ice
Dripping in oil
From the time spent in prayer
Hoping to attract the gold

Finding you
He hit the jackpot.
What attracted him was the God in you
He found a good thing.

A collection so attractive
Rooted in divine connection
No longer thirsting for traps
He obtained favor from you
This third cord it's priceless!

THE STRUGGLING FRIEND

I was struggling
                    I went to a friend
                                        She said:
Girl
    You gotta love yourself
    Just forgive and accept yourself

I'm gonna share what I wanted to say but kept to myself

Do you hear yourself?
Just spitting out the mantras of self-acceptance
As if it were an easy lesson
As if it were an easy prescription to take

For the vulnerable
It looks like a horse pill
That is not easy to swallow
Mistakes that came at a high cost
Are hard to forget
To forgive
To accept

Maybe you weren't such a dysfunctional mess
I can't dare say this aloud
It goes against the crowd
Negative Nancy is on repeat
You'll judge me that I've accepted defeat

I just want a little more compassion
For the lack of action
That isn't to your satisfaction
GIRL
Girl if you had a twirl into my wonderland
Maybe you'd understand

SUN MOON

Does the moon know about the sun
Is it jealous that the rays see more people
Than the crisp light in the night shade
Does it know how valuable it is
Nature's night light
Do the back roads look towards the concrete
The countryside isn't seeking city
So why do we do so much comparative living?
I want to hear the noise of my life and be content
Not be tossed to and fro comparing myself to highlight reels
I know it seems like nonsense
But take a sec
And you too
After a while start to get off track
Continuously looking on the opposite side of your facts

2020 TWO?

Renew
Refresh
Or is it just repeat?
Is it just me or do we need a beat?
I can't believe this sickness hit me twice
Feels like it's multiplied in size
The physical was felt and dealt with
But the long-lasting residual effects leave a mess
Mind games and tricks
Holding your breath from the anxiety and stress
Is it all vanity to chase success?

YOU ARE A GIFT

You are a gift
Rare like a ruby
Your perception is past skin deep
It's more than just shared stories and stats
You see beyond all that

You see the waves that crash against my soul
And despite the weather—the storms
You seek the pearls
Not the stones

Rubble everywhere yet all you see is the island
Palm trees that swayed yet were never broken
How do you see the words I've never spoken?

PERDÓN

El tiempo revela todo
Dice Mami
Pero esto yo no lo vi
El orgullo
El ego
Que vive en ti
No me deja dormir
La incapacidad de pedir disculpas
¿Qué tipo de amor no pide perdón nunca?
Dios ayúdame a perdonar
A perdonarme a mí misma
No quería verlo
Que el amor para mí no era cierto
La traición fue mía
Y en la memoria sigo sufriendo

MY FIRST TIME

The essence of you lingers
Like a ghost from Christmas past
They told me high school sweethearts never last
When memories come back to me
I can see the first-time love came to haunt me
I was 15
In turmoil and strife
Believing that a 16-year-old would someday make me his wife
It's funny
This life
I didn't know that I could love and lose in such magnitude
It was after September 11
I was a freshman
It was now October and the first fall party
I was feeling a bit older
Wore my new perfume
Your best friend introduced us
Yet it would be this same man that wanted to end us
The poetic letters of your aim messenger scribe
Made my heart skip a beat
In November you made sure
I would always remember this birth date
The roses and plans sharing dessert at Serendipity
Was like a movie scene
And on the last day of the year
Before the new year rang
I was yours and you were mine
I'd never forget my first time

TEEN DRAMA

I never had a boyfriend before
Or someone who loved me
But you believed that not even your love
Could cure the anger inside
That the love I needed only a dad could provide
While I drowned in sorrow you drowned in liquor
Your heart was slipping away from me like sand
Quicker and quicker
Words I did not know how to deliver
They were crass and loud
We argued and my friends got involved somehow
I never imagined that it would get you jumped
I was in a nightmare
A horror scene
When you got up
You looked at me
Disdain and hate was what I could calculate
I couldn't believe this was the end
How what I thought was fate
Came crashing down instead
20 years of life and experience later
I write down on paper
Romeo and Juliet
Tony and Maria
Benny and Nina
You and Me
It was a tragic story of
Love
Loss
As a teen

SOUL TIES

I want it
Without guilt

I want it
Without compromise

I want it
With love in your eyes

I want it
To be like worship

I want it
To last

I want it
To be blessed by God

I want it
For our souls to collide
For two to become one
To know you biblically and then some

BROKEN

I met him walking in my light   walking in my truth
His smile was like a mirror   blinding my own reflection
Our conversations made me feel safe
Our prayers took me higher

Yet I lost myself in him   putting him as number one
When I was ONE   my legs stayed closed

Protecting myself from all the misuse and abuse and pain
Inflicted from the bonding of my soul with those before

I thought I had to part the sea to keep him

                     And when I did...

I opened up the flood gates to a pain I didn't know was there

His smile
A facade
An act he played
He was in excruciating pain

       My light perpetuated that pain
       Posing as a mirror to his darkness
       Guess my mirror was BROKEN too

                     How did I get here again?

Identifying myself in this black man
Wanting to lick his wounds
Erase his pain
All while inflicting so much on myself!

       Yet this pattern isn't new
       Its familiar to you—
       Your Mother did it
       Your Grandmother did it
       And so many women before.

       GENERATIONAL BROKENESS
       HOW DO I GET WHOLE?

ROTA (Broken in Spanish)

Lo conocí caminando en mi luz   caminando en mi verdad
Su sonrisa fue como un espejo   cegando mi propio reflejo
Nuestras conversaciones me hicieron sentir segura
Nuestras oraciones me llevaron más alto

Sin embargo me perdí en él   poniéndolo como número uno
Cuando yo era UNA   mis piernas se mantuvieron cerradas

Protegiéndome de todo el maltrato   abuso y dolor
Infligido por la unión de mi alma con aquellos antes

Yo pensé que tenía que separar el mar para mantenerlo

Y cuando lo hice abrí las puertas a un dolor que no sabía que estaba allí

Su sonrisa
Una fachada
Un acto que interpretó
Él estaba en un dolor insoportable

      Mi luz perpetuó ese dolor
        Posando como un espejo a su oscuridad
        Supongo que mi espejo también estaba ROTO

            ¿Cómo llegué aquí de nuevo?

Identificándome en este hombre negro
Queriendo lamer sus heridas
Borraré su dolor
¡Todo mientras me infringía tanto!

     Sin embargo
     Este patrón no es nuevo
     Es familiar para ti—
     Tu madre lo hizo
     Tu abuela lo hizo
     Y tantas mujeres antes

     QUEBRANTAMIENTO GENERACIONAL
     ¿CÓMO ME VUELVO ENTERA?

LOVE WRITES HERE

When Love didn't show up
The words did

      The capacity to bring alliteration
      To the obliteration of my heart brought shalom

As the ultimate love brought healing
I started reeling
Where did my words go?
I started feeling you
For real
That's when the truth began to be revealed
You chose me even when I didn't choose you
That reflection of your intention
Towards me
Left me breathless

                                   Acceptance

That was next
Believing that Love was looking right at me
Could the words reflect the test

To rise and not fall
To be Love
To show Love
To page
And not erase

Showing up to the page
Meant Love
Four letters
Start there
Believe you are meant to be where
Love prevails
Love attests
And Love provides the rest
The light
The strength
To be all of what you were created to be

You were created to create
Don't take the bait
Love doesn't lie or change its mind
Love said what it said

You are chosen

                                        Elegida

You are worthy

                                        Valiosa

And no matter the mess
Love writes here

GOD DON'T PLAY ABOUT ME

I tried to tell him
The God I serve
Don't play about me
I pray to the Lord reveal every hidden thing
So what you thought you got away with
My prayers lead your demons to snitch
Ain't that about a blip
The old me would have used a different B
For that word
But God has been working on curving that urge
Instead of the curse
I am here to serve
Serve goodness and grace
And for those who betray my case
He said no need for my voice to raise
Vengeance is mine
I will deal with them in time
So go about your day
Because continuing to serve me
Everything will be added on to you
You'll see

WRITE YOUR OWN VOWS

I chased and chased and chased
Wanting to be chosen
Wanting to be loved

I'm ready for radical change
A radical start

I vow to not look for love but be love
I vow to not compromise myself for your acceptance
I vow to say NO
I vow to choose joy
I vow to honor the light in me and not dim it to please
I vow to be kind in spite of the cruelty in the world
I vow to smile because my teeth are not for your commercial comfort
I vow to be present because my past does not define me
I vow to create to leave behind a legacy
I vow to fight for my happiness and not expect it to come from you
I vow to let you add to the recipe but not take away the vital ingredients
I vow to rejoice when I set healthy boundaries
I vow to relinquish control when I can't do anything to change my
circumstance
I vow to surrender to a purpose that is greater so that love can cast out
all fears!

NOW WRITE YOUR OWN VOWS:

LOVE   **LIES**   **HERE**

BETWEEN THE GUILT OF YOUR SHAME

THE BURDEN OF YOUR PAIN

LOVE   LIES   HERE

YOUR SELF-SABATOGE   WORKING AGAINST YOURSELF

MASTERING THE NOBODY LOVES ME SPEECH

LOVE LIES HERE

EVEN WHEN YOU DON'T SEE IT

EVEN WHEN YOU DON'T FEEL IT

LOVE IS HERE

CHAPTER 4

GOD AND TRUTH

God
Are you there?
It's me
Celi
Feeling like Judy Bloom some days
Or is it that I wish I could give some Godly truth
To the girl who read those books
Why do people hate you so much
So in turn they hate me?
I do my best and get burned at the stake
While their sins seem to go Scot-free
I know I just talked about the lies
And you are the way the light and the truth
Reality is this is harder than I want it to
Your answers aren't always what I want to hear
But let me be clear
You have always looked out for my good
I've wanted to renegotiate the terms of my
representation So many times
Ridiculous I know
To think I know better than you
Get me out of my own way
To live a life that represents you
GOD

GOD DREAM

This is a GOD Dream
It had to be
I ran to the page
When I had no place to go
Then I ran away—
Not wanting to be swayed
by the foundation my father had laid
But I had to stop looking down
at his steps and look up and see the steps ordered
Steps ordained to cross
My disobedience came with a cost

I paid the price of insecurity
       Wrapped in unforgiveness

Disillusioned with thoughts of unworthiness
     Big shoes to fill
And then
      I got STILL
Began to rest
In the promises you said you would fulfill
You promised hope
So here I am again at the page
Hoping you heal this pacer that was placed

By all the heartaches that have been difficult to erase
I will write the vision and make it plain
I want the peace to walk
In my GOD DREAM

CAMBIÉ

¡Ay
Si tú pudieras entender!
I know it's hard to comprehend

Del día a la noche cambié
I could try to tell you cómo fue

You're just gonna think it's religiosa mess
Entonces
¿Cómo te digo lo que me hizo?

The encounter I had with
El Espíritu Santo

I was minding my business
In praise and worship
Cuando mi boca
Comenzó a tener mente propia

I thought it was all for show
Cosas que asumí
Más cuando yo me comprometí
Ahí es cuando te sentí

It was heavy the weight of
¡La Gloria!

Y hablé un lenguaje
que no tiene palabras

A holy language
And it wasn't Spanish

Me cambió por dentro
Its like I had heart surgery

Pero no stitches
Me sanó de lo que no puedes ver

That's why you don't understand
You can't see his hand

Esa mano que nunca deja mi lado
es magia más allá de cualquier humano

GRACE

What can I tell you
About how I hold space for you
Grace

Betrayal of another doesn't make it safe for
Grace

My courteous goodwill
Comes from the hope he instilled
Usually there would be holes I would drill
Find crevices & cracks to break you
Grace

But the free and unmerited
Favor of God that saved me
Changed me
No longer retaliation
Grace

Not my own vindication
Grace

Not playing judge nor jury
Grace

Mistakes erased
Given a clean slate
Grace

It was done for me
So when I gave it to you
It wasn't about you

It was about GRACE

DEEP

If deep calls to the deep
Then the evidence of what
I see must mean
Too many don't know how to swim
Let me not judge
Maybe they prefer shallow waters
Less work
They get to stay cute and seen
For the appearance of their physique
Going deep
Well that exposes
The strength of their core
The lack of their faith
And all the places they hid for their escape
Going deep
Requires all of you
Not part of you

MEMORIES

Your memories have no borders
There can be a lot of disorder in that
They come and go as they please
Why do you remember the sadness
More than the joy
In the shadows of the life dance
Is that where your joy got stuck
I know the crawl space of the darkness
Has become homey
There's light and joy on the other side
Just follow me
I know it's hard to understand
Just look at the plan at hand
I too went into a dark space
And then I rose again
You can let some memories die
While others will resurrect

AWARD

Accolade
A special honor
What does it mean?
Now I'm special?
Better?
I think not
I feel joy to be seen by this talent machine
I feel honored to represent for the most-high king

But what I don't get
Is when you feel unworthy if the merit is never met
Acknowledged
Remembered

                           Yet what do I know

What do WE know?
Solace
Is what we seek
Speak

The consultation for the madness
The sadness
There is an admiration
For the consideration
Of being embraced

Oh the praise!
Praise of my peers
Praise of my wildest fears
It can be intoxicatedly dangerous

Sucked into believing your worthiness is tied up in it
Getting high on your own supply

Yet when you go home you don't feel
What you thought you would
You were chasing a feeling instead of a reason
Now your soul is bleeding
And you didn't even really receive it

The real reward

Remember who deserves all the praise
Not me

                 G!

Go put some respect on the name

                 O!

Or be reminded of its power

                 D!

Don't mistake the accolade is great

Just remember who put the blessing on your plate

FROM MY PAIN

I've been writing from my pain
Writing from my shame
So it feels strange to look at the empty page
To write with hope

How do I begin to layer away
What your love has done for me
I didn't really believe it was possible
I thought I was asking for the impossible
Feeling undesirable,
Too much
But you saw it as a place that God said level up

Now I'm stuck
Like my feet are glued to this space
The space you made
In the traffic jam of my heart
Even being miles apart
I feel you close
God keeps you far enough from me
To keep me
Knowing that the distance
Would keep the discipline of resistance
But no matter what
I'm just thankful for your existence

SPOKEN LANGUAGE

Finding recourse
For you to become familiar to me
For me to favor you
And for you to favor me
My favorite was your opposite
NO objections
Fearing rejection
I downplayed you
And commenced with my YES
YES was the chaser
To the bitter taste of abandonment
And laced with lack of love of self

I want a NO
To know
That's where the boundary lies
It's where my spirit will begin to fly

WHAT AM I RESISTING

I resisted you for so long
If you were a man
I'd say you were a bug-a-boo
Even when I cursed you
Even when I said I didn't want to follow you
I resisted you
Resisted your words—
That transformed nations because of man's manipulation
I've heard you set people free but again man's greed
Used it to keep us caged
Enslaved
I had more than one encounter
More than one save
Of feeling your love
Your grace

I kept on running
Hard-headed I know
It runs in the veins
Still you stayed
Patient and kind
My ignorance you didn't mind
You were laughing the whole time
Knowing that the path to you I would eventually find
I didn't know what you knew
I wouldn't have believed you anyway

That you would choose a loud-mouth
Swearing,
A whole lotta livin'
Not even grown up in it as your mouth piece
So as I prepare to go minister to your people
Now I laugh at my own resistance
You never left me
Nor forsaked me
Thank you God that you never left me

MY TEACHER

Haven't quite figured it out yet
Why pain is the best teacher?
Why can't sunsets at beaches
reach the inner depths of places
Or the satisfaction
Of finally learning to tie my shoelaces?

You remember that?
Nope
Me either

I remember the exhaustion
The sick and tired moments of being sick and tired
The betrayal of the liar

That time I got fired

Those are the memories
and soliloquies that play out like a symphony
Displaying the growth and depth
Of the life that was full of pains I can't regret

How could you?
How could I?
When that pain became our reasons why

Why we rose
After we fell
How we are still standing
With our stories to tell

WHO DO I PRAY FOR?

Who do I pray for?
I pray for you
In the morning light
Yet sometimes
The spirit wakes me up at night

At 4am your soul is knocking at my bedpost

Its Fine
Okay Fine...
It's not fine...

(Deep Sighs)

I pray you grow up inside
There is a lot of pain you hide
Praying you remove your costume of pride
It sticks to you like skin so you can't even see the lie
I pray the truth hits you like a bat to your knee caps

Don't judge my prayer
Every knee shall bow
Including yours
And sometimes my God's a little ratchet
You know

TRAUMA

It keeps coming up
It's working against my promise
Seek love first not trauma

NO VES

No sé bien la respuesta
¿Cómo enseñarte lo que no ves?
Tu valor es invisible
Tu valor es esencial
Tu amor es esencial
Pero no lo ves
No ves que no es la voluntad de Dios
No es eso
No es ese abuso
No es el uso de ti e esa manera

Jesús volteó las mesas cuando vio el lío de la gente
¿Entonces por qué te sientas en la mesa como el sacrificio ?

MADE

Pruned to make wine
Bent to make chocolate
Cut to make diamond

Imagine what it took to make you

THE PLACE

You ever left a place
And it keeps pulling you back?
Una cosa es de donde tu vienes
and another thing is where you are called
Si
Soy de alla
Pero este ambiente
No es para mí alimento
I'm letting go of the toxicity
Of the familiar environments
From where I came from
Reaching higher
Wanted to make way
Para la generación que viene
Para la generación que me jala

SITTING AT THE DOCK

Sitting at the dock
I do not want to be left behind
The boat is approaching
And I know what I'm carrying is too heavy to hide
This cargo is not allowed inside
You said no condemnation aboard
To look towards you and we will not drown
The shame and guilt of my choices
Are trying to anchor me
To this land and keep me ten toes down
Your faith in me says I can shed it and walk on water
I'm fighting the fear to not drown and wallow
It became a familiar and conversation starter
I want to walk on water!
I want to leave it all behind
And walk with my head held high
Knowing that for all of it your son died

PREACHER GIRL

You're a preacher girl?
How sway?
I remember you from back in the day

You're really waiting
Until you are wed?

What if that D is wack?
You'll keep that for life?

I wouldn't risk it
Jesus knows my life

He knows yours too and you still don't have a ring?
How's that working out for you Queen?

                    God is working all things together for my good

I mean ARE you good
Without the wood?
This is the thing about church girls I never understood

                 I have peace that surpasses your understanding

                Not returning to my own vomit thinking about all
                    The times I cast my pearls before swine
                                     Yea
                            I'm good
I would have never thought you would turn out this way

Then again maybe I would

                 Before I was formed I was known and became
                 What he already knew if you got to know him
                 Maybe you would too

STOP AND STARE

Comparison robs your joy
So
Guess where I've been
Hiding somewhere
Ducking the thief that comes to steal it
Hiding from the matrix
Wanting to reveal it
The place where the real me lies
Without the need of the likes
Without the addiction
Of the transfixion of your stare
Without the desire to grow in numbers
Instead of depth
Discovering to find the things
I don't know about myself just yet
Like how less tangled my mind would be
The clearer I'd see
And more connected to real life I'd be
So
I'm standing here present
Hesitant
About where my career might be
I want to be an artist that's free
From chasing after the approval of the masses
Just to eat
I want to stand firm in truth
That provision isn't
In the glare of the screen
But in the decision to choose
His vision over yours

BELIEVER

Teaching

        Preaching

                Reaching

Reaching for spaces and places

      I'm still trying to find

             Searching for joy

Searching for peace

    Searching for the why it cannot be

     Are the dreams too far from my reach

Don't sell out for the dream

      Don't stop

           Don't quit

    I have a story to live!

WOMAN AT THE WELL

There is a story to tell
About a woman at a well
She has a story but to no one she would tell

A man approached her and was kind
Asked her for some water
And she couldn't understand why

She believed the stories spread about her
Lies became truth
And although her father was trying to find her
Abandonment is the only truth she knew

Searching for love in all the wrong spaces
Created brokenness that now lives in her heart
That asking her for water made her snap
Out of the abundance of that heart
Her mouth speaks
"Why are you talking to me?"

Her vision was blurred about this kind man
Because her vision was blurred about herself
If she knew the gift of his kindness
And the life it would give
Imagine the joy she could live

SIFTING

Sifting and shifting
Moving from sand to rock
Not losing my balance like before
When the storms come
I got knocked down and got back up
Started building back the pieces
Of what the storm blew away

TRUTH

I never really had a diary
I couldn't stay consistent in my writing
Poems became the diary
Then Poems became the blog
Then poems became a book?
Will anyone read it?
Will anyone care?
Will people get it?
Can't allow the fear of failure
Get in my way
Or maybe I'm in the way of my success
My busyness is being addressed
God sat me down
God saw me
       Running
                Running
                         Running

Myself ragged
Stretching myself thin
How with such faith do I have such mistrust?
That God will do it in his time
So what's mine I won't miss

Dear Diary
Dear Reader
Now I will rest
Now that the words
On the page and spaces between
Have a beautiful meaning

I'm enough
I've passed the test

ACKNOWLEDGMENTS

Thank you to God, the creator who created me to create. For all the gifts I have been blessed with including the village that helped make this book happen. I dedicate this book to all of you.

I give honor and thanks to my late father Dr. Francisco Chapman-Veloz author and poet.

My mother, Santa Varela, who allowed me to give life to words she didn't always have.

My Chapman siblings- Quetzachual, Vantroi, Maireni, Kamal, Francisco, and Chris Imani who supported this journey and the publication of our father's poem.

First eyes to read: Essence Atkins and Julissa Calderon, both saw the birth of my book baby and handled it with such care, joy, and love.

My prayer warrior Tecoya Harris who held me up in the spirit and reminded me that I AM AN AUTHOR.

My editor Roxana Calderón, your prayers, love, and hard work helped make this dream a reality.

Book Cover artist AnaMelissa you took an idea I had an elevated to the next level! Your attention to incorporate the life in my poems into this hand-painted masterpiece is what makes me love my cover so much!

Alegria Publishing/Davina Ferreria for seeing my talent and giving me the scholarship for the writing classes that birthed this collection.

Dominican Writers and Angy Abreu for their unwavering support, guidance, and always championing my work.

ABOUT THE AUTHOR

Franceli Chapman-Varela is an award-winning Afro-Latina Actor. Born on the island of Dominican Republic, she migrated to America illegally with her mother at the age of 3. Now an American Citizen, Franceli has added many titles to her name. Between Spaces is Ms. Chapman's debut poetry collection.

She began writing poetry as a child as a form of self-expression when she didn't have the words for what she was experiencing. Inspired by her late father who was also a writer/poet, she deferred the dream to write, afraid of the big shoes to fill but she made her own path. Franceli went on to perform off-off Broadway theater starting in high school, and her play, A Work in Progress was produced at the Castillo Theater as part of the Young Playwrights Festival. Her short story, "A Runner's Heart" was featured in Audible book: "Talking while Female and Other Dangerous Acts" Franceli has covered and written for Houston Style Magazine, Broadway Black, Soul Essence Magazine and has been featured in the NY TIMES, Amsterdam News, CNN, and Telemunco.

When Franceli is not on Film/TV, stage or writing you can find her preaching, hiking or belting karaoke tunes. She currently resides in Los Angeles, California.

More info at www.celihangout.com